THE HISTORY
OF MUSIC
AND CINEMA

EVALUATION PART I

THE HISTORY OF MUSIC AND CINEMA

Evaluation Part I

Ali Zokaee

Printed in the United States of America

ISBN 979-8-89114-112-4 (sc)
ISBN 979-8-89114-113-1 (hc)
ISBN 979-8-89114-114-8 (e)

Library of Congress Control Number: 2024916299

2024.11.04

MainSpring Books
5901 W. Century Blvd
Suite 750
Los Angeles, CA, US, 90045

www.mainspringbooks.com

PREFACE

Music and cinema used to be the main drivers of cultural movements in the second half of the 20th century. They don't have that important impact anymore. They are 20th century phenomena. This book is an evaluation of the reader's knowledge about the history of music and cinema when they were the most influential cultural shaping tools.

There are 12 chapters in this book which the first 6 comprise of the questions about the history of music, and the second 6 about the history of cinema. Each chapter has 30 questions which the reader should be able to finish in 45 minutes. The questions are not analytical, so you either know the answer or you don't. Also, the questions come in different levels of difficulty. There are easy questions, moderately difficult questions, and difficult questions.

If you answer less than 10 questions correctly in each chapter, the level of your knowledge is considered as low. If you answer somewhere between 10 to 19 questions correctly in each chapter, the level of your knowledge is considered as medium, and if you answer more than 20 questions correctly in each chapter, the level of your knowledge is considered as high about the subjects.

After taking each test, you can start reading and learning about the questions that you either didn't know the answer, or you answered incorrectly. This way, you learn a lot about the history of music and cinema after each test which will be quite enjoyable for anyone who is interested in these topics.

It is better to take each test on a separate day following a few days of studying. This way you get a comprehensive benefit of the book rather than just going through questions. If you are just interested or knowledgeable about music, you can just focus on the first six chapters. Also, if you are just interested or knowledgeable about cinema, chapters 7 to 12 are suitable for you.

I hope you learn a lot about these subjects and questions after finishing the book and hopefully enjoy the ride.

CHAPTER 1

1. In the 1976 "Eric Clapton's" album "No Reason To Cry", he duets one of the songs with "Bob Dylan". What's the name of that song ?

2. Who wrote these two hit songs ? "Beautiful" by "Christina Aguilera", and "Get The Party Started" by "Pink".

3. "Eric Clapton" played the lead guitar on one of the songs in "White Album" by "The Beatles" in 1968. What song was that ?

4. Which "Steely Dan" album had "Mark Knopfler" as lead guitarist on one of the songs ?

5. This song was first performed in 1966 by "The Supremes", then in 1967 by the "Vanilla Fudge" and in 1986 by "Kim Wilde". What's the title of the song ?

6. In 1990 "Mc Hammer" released the single "U Can't Touch This" which sampled one of the songs by "Rick James". What's the title of that song ?

7. In 1970s, "Alan Parsons" started the "Alan Parsons Project" as a duo. What is the name of his band mate ?

8. He is considered as one of the most powerful Blues and R&B vocalists which released three live albums alongside "B.B. King" in 1974, 1976 and 1987.

9. In 1971 three band members of this British blues band left their original band, formed "Foghat", relocated to U.S. and signed to "Bearsville Records". What is the name of their original band ?

10. What is the name of "John Lennon and Yoko Ono's" backing band in 1972 for the "Some Time In New York City" album ?

11. In November of 1969, four of one of the record company executives went to "Birmingham" to see two bands, and they signed one of them. The band that they signed was "Black Sabbath". What is the name of the other band ?

12. Even though he started as a trumpet player in 1960s and released several albums in that decade, but he is one of the richest people in music industry as the co-founder of "A&M Records".

13. After "Sam Phillips" rejected "Elvis Presley" once, he came back and in 1954 sang a song outside of the "Sun Records" which made "Sam Phillips" change his mind and signed him to "Sun Records". Which Blues singer did "Elvis Presley" cover that day ?

14. Right before he released his first solo album in 1971, "Billy Joel" with one of his band mates released a self-titled psychedelic album in 1970. What is the title of that album ?

15. Which psychedelic band featured "Phil Collins" before he joined "Genesis" in 1970 ? The band released one album in 1969 called "Ark 2".

16. In 1967, "Hurtin'" was released as a single by the Garage Rock band featuring "Don Henley". What is the name of that band ?

17. In 1978 "Whitesnake" included the heavy metal version of "Ain't No Love In The Heart Of The City" in their "Snakebite" album. Who recorded the R&B version of this song 4 years prior to that in 1974 ?

18. One of the most prolific Blues songwriters of the 1950s with compositions like: "Hoochie Coochie Man", "I Can't Quit You Baby", "Back Door Man", and "Spoonful".

19. On how many "Bob Dylan" albums did "Mark Knopfler" play guitar ?

20. Which one of these musicians doesn't belong to the "27 Club" ?
    A. Robert Johnson
    B. Ian Curtis
    C. Amy Winehouse
    D. Kurt Cobain
    E. Janis Joplin
    F. Jim Morrison
    G. Jimi Hendrix
    H. Brian Jones

21. In 1978 "Judas Priest" recoded their version of "Better By You, Better Than Me" in the "Stained Class" album. Which band recorded the original version of this song in 1969 ?

22. Who wrote the song "Hang On To A Dream" that was featured in the album "Nice" by "The Nice" ?

23. In 1978 "Stevie Ray Vaughan" formed his band "Double Trouble", which he named after a song by a reputable bluesman. Who was that bluesman ?

24. Which band did "Gary Brooker" and "Robin Trower" play together before forming "Procol Harum" ?

25. Almost a decade before starting his solo career, Which band did "Gary Moore" join as a guitarist in late 1960s as his first band to play in ?

26. Which song was performed by these three women: "Etta James", "Christine Perfect", and "Beth Hart" ?

27. Before they call themselves "Simon & Garfunkel" in 1964, the duo had a different name since 1957. What was the original name of the duo ?

28. While playing as a session guitarist from 1959 to 1968 in "Chess Records", "Leonard Chess" the Founder of "Chess Records" refused to record him the way he plays and kept him as a session guitarist for backing "Muddy Waters", "Howlin' Wolf", "Sonny Boy Williamson" and others. What is the name of this guitar player ?

29. This "R.E.M." and "Warren Zevon" collaboration resulted in one self-titled album in 1990. What is the name of that band ?

30. In 1967 in the album "United", "Marvin Gaye" alongside one other singer sang the first version of "Ain't No Mountain High Enough". Who accompanied him to sing this song ?

CHAPTER 2

1. Which of these bands didn't have "Ronnie James Dio" as a member ?
   A. Whitesnake
   B. Black Sabbath
   C. Elf
   D. Rainbow

2. "Ronnie Van Zant" founded "Lynyrd Skynyrd". "Johnny Van Zant" founded "Johnny Van Zant Band". What is the name of the band that the third brother "Donnie Van Zant" founded ?

3. After leaving "Yardbirds", he formed "Renaissance" in late 1960s which featured his sister too. Then he joined "Armageddon" and after releasing their only album in 1975, he accidentally passed away a year later in 1976.

4. He formed two New Wave bands in 1976 and 1977, "Buzzcocks" and "Magazine". Then started his solo career in 1983. What is his name ?

5. What was the name of "Don Henley's" band which released one self titled Country Rock album in 1970 before forming "The Eagles" the next year ?

6. After "Blind Faith" disbanded in 1969, "Eric Clapton" joined this duo band before releasing his first solo album in 1970. What is the name of that band ?

7. What was the name of the Folk band that "Kenny Rogers" joined in 1966 before forming "The First Edition" a year later in 1967 ?

8. In 1974 this Scottish Blues Rock singer started her solo career with the album "Queen Of The Night". What is the name of the band that she was in from 1970 to 1973 ?

9. After leaving "Electric Light Orchestra", which band did "Roy Wood" founded in 1972 ?

10. In 1969, "Harry Nilsson" sang "Everybody's Talking" in the soundtrack of the movie "Midnight Cowboy". Who wrote this song ?

11. Who was "Buddy Guy's" companion during late 1960s and throughout 1970s whom they released six albums together ?

12. The influential and powerful vocalist of "Strawbs" and "Fairport Convention" before releasing her solo debut "The North Star Grassman And The Ravens" in 1971 ?

13. In the 1985 album "Showdown!", "Albert Collins" and "Robert Cray" collaborated with this third guitarist. What is his name ?

14. Which drummer was the member of these following bands: "Rainbow", "Whitesnake", "Black Sabbath", and "Jeff Beck Group" ?

15. Which one of these bands didn't include at least one member of "ELP (Emerson, Lake & Palmer)" ?
    A. Atomic Rooster
    B. Nice
    C. King Crimson
    D. Asia
    E. The Crazy World Of Arthur Brown
    F. Mind Garage

16. Which one of these "Rolling Stones" albums doesn't feature "Mick Taylor" as guitarist ?
    A. Beggars Banquet (1968)
    B. Let It Bleed (1969)
    C. Sticky Fingers (1971)
    D. Exile On Main Street (1972)
    E. Goats Head Soup (1973)
    F. It's Only Rock 'N' Roll (1974)

17. Which one of these songs is not in the album "Revolver (1966)" by "The Beatles" ?
    A. Taxman
    B. Eleanor Rigby
    C. Here, There And Everywhere
    D. Nowhere Man
    E. Good Day Sunshine
    F. For No One

18. What was the first album released by "Doobie Brothers" that featured "Michael McDonald" ?

19. "Eric Clapton" considers him as one of his biggest influences and the guitarist "Who taught me how to make love to a guitar". Who's that guitarist ?

20. The singer for the first three "Deep Purple" albums which was replaced by "Ian Gillian" in 1969. Which band did he join in 1972 and released two albums with them ?

21. What is the name of the band that "Roger Glover" and "Ian Gillan" were in, before joining "Deep Purple" in 1969 ?

22. Which one of these musicians were not a member of "Deep Purple" ?
    A. Steve Morse
    B. Tommy Bolin
    C. Glenn Hughes
    D. Ronnie James Dio
    E. David Coverdale

23. The song "The Hunter" which was on the 1969 album with the same title by "Ike & Tina Turner", two years prior to that was performed by this musician in his 1967 album. What is the name of that musician ?

24. "With A Little Help From His Friends" he released his solo debut album and also his self-titled second album both in 1969. What is the name of this singer ?

25. Which one of these "Beatles" songs was written by "Ringo Starr" ?
    A. Yellow Submarine
    B. Eleanor Rigby
    C. Norwegian Wood
    D. The Fool On The Hill
    E. Octopus's Garden
    F. Lucy In The Sky With Diamonds

26. In 1988 "Traveling Wilburys" released their debut album. Other than "George Harrison", "Bob Dylan", "Tom Petty" and "Roy Orbison", who was the fifth member of the supergroup ?

27. Which one of these was not a member of the band "The Highwaymen" which released their first album called "Highwayman" in 1985 and their last album "The Road Goes On Forever" in 1995 ?
    A. Bob Dylan
    B. Kris Kristofferson
    C. Johnny Cash
    D. Waylon Jennings
    E. Willie Nelson

28. What is the name of the band that was active from 1967 to 1970 and released three albums in 1968, 1969, and 1970 featuring "Bob Seger" before he formed "Bob Seger & The Silver Bullet Band" in 1974 ?

29. Which drummer was the member of all of these bands throughout his career: "Jeff Beck Group", "The Mothers Of Invention", "John Mayall & The Bluesbreakers", "Jefferson Starship", "Journey", and "Whitesnake" ?

30. Which "B.B. King" album featured "Ringo Starr" on drums ?

CHAPTER 3

1. What is the title of the last "Diana Ross & The Supremes" album before "Diana Ross" left the band ?

2. What is the title of the first song that "Elvis Presley" recorded in 1953 ?

3. Before changing their name to "The Supremes" in 1961, what was the name of that band in 1959 and 1960 ?

4. The band members of "Commodores" came together from two different bands after they disbanded. One of those bands was "The Mystics", what was the other band ?

5. In early 1960s which future Folk Rock superstar was a member of the Doo Wop band "The Mystics" ?

6. What was the name of the band in 1968 when all main four members formed the first incarnation of the band before changing its name the next year to "Black Sabbath" ?

7. Which one of these female soul singers didn't collaborate with "Marvin Gaye" ?
   A. Aretha Franklin
   B. Tammi Terrell
   C. Mary Wells
   D. Kim Weston
   E. Diana Ross

8. What is the title of the last album that "Richard Thompson" recorded with "Fairport Convention" as a member before his departure ?

9. The dissolution of which band in late 1960s resulted in the formation of "Caravan" and "Soft Machine" ?

10. What is the title of the first non-R&B album that "Moody Blues" released and changed the direction of their music afterwards ?

11. What is the name of the band that "Robert Wyatt" formed in 1971 after leaving "Soft Machine" which also included "Dave Sinclair" from "Caravan" ?

12. "Ray Charles'" first top ten R&B single was "Baby, Let Me Hold Your Hand" in 1951. What is the title of his first top ten Pop single in 1959 ?

13. What is the title of the first "Chuck Berry" single that was released in 1955 ?

14. Which band released these albums: "Face To Face (1966)", "The Village Green Preservation Society (1968)", "Arthur (Or The Decline And Fall Of The British Empire (1969)", and "Muswell Hillbillies (1971)" ?

15. What was the name of "Creedence Clearwater Revival" from 1964 to 1967 before they changed it to "CCR" ?

16. What is the first "Genesis" album featuring "Phil Collins" ?

17. What is the last "Genesis" album featuring "Peter Gabriel" before his first departure ?

18. Which band did "Robert Fripp" play in before forming "Giles, Giles & Fripp" in 1967 ?

19. Before starting his solo career in 1984, which band was "Vince Gill" a member from 1979 to 1981 ?

20. In 1989 which band offered "Vince Gill" to become full time member, but he declined because of the success of his solo album "When I Call Your Name (1989)" ?

21. Who was the first artist to release a Long Playing album with "Sun Records" in 1957 ?

22. Which band did "Roger Chapman" form after "Family" ?

23. What was the name of the band that "Carole King" alongside her then husband founded in 1968 before starting her solo career ?

24. Which guitarist played piano alongside his band on "Rocket 88" by "Jackie Brenston" in 1951 produced by "Sam Phillips" ?

25. Which one of these bands was not the part of "Detroit Rock" scene in late 1960s, early 1970s ?
    A. The Amboy Dukes
    B. Frijid Pink
    C. MC5
    D. Blue Cheer
    E. The Stooges
    F. Brownsville Station
    G. Grand Funk Railroad

26. What was the name of the Psychedelic band that "J.J. Cale" founded in 1966 before starting his solo career ?

27. Before starting his solo career, "Chris Rea" was performing with a band called "Magdalene" which he replaced their singer. Who was that singer ?

28. Who wrote the song "Polk Salad Annie" which "Elvis Presley" was performing it in his "Las Vegas" shows ?

29. Which one of these musicians did not record with "Sam Phillips" of "Sun Records" ?
    A. Howlin' Wolf
    B. Bobby "Blue" Bland
    C. Little Milton
    D. Rufus Thomas
    E. Conway Twitty
    F. Willie Nelson
    G. Johnny Cash
    H. Roy Orbison
    I. Carl Perkins
    J. Jerry Lee Lewis
    K. B.B. King

30. In which "Bob Dylan" album was "Johnny Cash" a guest star ?

CHAPTER 4

1. Which one of these bands "David Coverdale" was not a member of ?
   A. Whitesnake
   B. Deep Purple
   C. Rainbow
   D. The Government
   E. The Fabulosa Brothers

2. Who was the singer of "Deep Purple" in late 1960s and of "Captain Beyond" in the 1970s ?

3. In 1962 "Bo Diddley" had a hit song called "You Can't Judge A Book By It's Cover". Who wrote that song ?

4. Which one of these musicians didn't record with "Chess Records" ?
   A. Howlin' Wolf
   B. B.B. King
   C. Bo Diddley
   D. Willie Dixon
   E. Chuck Berry
   F. Muddy Waters
   G. Buddy Guy
   H. John Lee Hooker

5. Before forming "Spooky Tooth" what was the name of the band that "Mike Harrison" was a member of from 1965 to 1967 before they changed their name to "Art" ?

6. Which "Soft Machine" member founded the band "Gong" in 1967 ?

7. Which one of these bands is not considered as a part of the "Canterbury Scene" genre ?
    A. Soft Machine
    B. Caravan
    C. Gong
    D. Matching Mole
    E. The Strawbs

8. What was the last album of "James Gang" that featured "Joe Walsh" on guitar ?

9. What was the name of the Psychedelic Rock band that was formed in 1965 in Long Island, New York before they changed their name to "Vanilla Fudge" in 1967 ?

10. What was the name of the band that "Wilson Pickett" was its singer in late 1950s early 1960s before starting his solo career ?

11. Which Alternative band from Cincinnati, OH released the album "Gentlemen" in 1993 ?

12. In 1974 album by the eagles "On The Border" they covered one of the songs from the first "Tom Waits" album "Closing Time (1973)". What is the title of that song ?

13. In 1990 "Jonathan Donahue" was playing guitar for two bands for releasing their upcoming albums. One of those bands was "Flaming Lips". What was the other band ?

14. What was the name of the Australian band in late 1970s before they change their name to "Birthday Party" in 1980 ?

15. In 1971 album "Hold On, It's Coming" by "Country Joe McDonald", which British guitarist play ?

16. In which "Lucinda Williams" album did "Rick Rubin" collaborate with her ?

17. After leaving "The Rolling Stones" which band did "Dick Taylor" form in 1963 ?

18. In which year was "Joan Baez" invited to perform at the "Newport Folk Festival" as a solo artist for the first time ?

19. After leaving "Jethro Tull" in November 1968, which band did "Mick Abrahams" form ?

20. What is the title of the first "Fleetwood Mac" album featuring this line up: "Mike Fleetwood", "Christine Perfect", "John McVie", "Lindsey Buckingham", and "Stevie Nicks" ?

21. What is the name of the last band that "Keith Relf" was a member of, before his death in 1976 ?

22. What was the name of the band "The Kinks" prior to 1964 ?

23. Which band did "Sandy Denny" form after leaving "Fairport Convention" in 1970 and before starting her solo career in 1971 ?

24. Which British Blues Rock band played as the backing band in 1966 "John Lee Hooker" album "Seven Nights" ?

25. Who sang the first version of the song "A Nickel And A Nail" in 1971 and then released it in his 1972 album "A Nickel And A Nail And Ace Of Spades" ?

26. What is the title of the last "The Byrds" album that featured "David Crosby" ?

27. What was the first "The Rolling Stones" album that they released on their own label "Rolling Stones Records" ?

28. What is the title of the "John Mayall And The Blues Breakers" album that "Peter Green" plays guitar in ?

29. What was the last "Fleetwood Mac" album that "Jeremy Spencer" appeared on before he joined the religious group "Children Of God" ?

30. What was the name of the band that "Leslie West" was playing guitar in, from 1965 to 1968 before he formed "Mountain" ?

Chapter 5

1. In 1977 album "Foreign Affairs" by "Tom Waits" he co sings the song "I Never Talk To Strangers" with which other singer as a duet ?

2. What is the title of the first "The Rolling Stones" album with all original songs without any cover ?

3. What is the title of the last "Joan Baez" album that was issued by "Vanguard" ?

4. What is the title of the first "Jethro Tull" album that was released on "Chrysalis" ?

5. What is the title of the first album by "The Kinks" that they released for RCA after the expiration of their contract with "Pye/Reprise" in 1971 ?

6. What is the title of the only album by "Uriah Heep" that "John Wetton" played Base Guitar on as a band member ?

7. What is the name of the band that existed for a year from 1965 to 1966 in Los Angeles with "Taj Mahal" and "Ry Cooder" as band members ?

8. What is the title of the first album that "Them" released after "Van Morrison" departure ?

9. In which "Bob Dylan" album, "Michael Bloomfield" played electric guitar ?

10. What was the name of the "Grateful Dead" prior to 1965 ?

11. Who was the "The Jimi Hendrix Experience" bassist who left the band in 1968 and formed "Fat Mattress" which released two albums in 1969 and 1970 ?

12. In which "Tom Petty & The Heartbreakers" album did "Bob Dylan" work with them ?

13. What is the title of the first number one single by "Neil Young" ?

14. In 1996 album "The Score" by "Fugees", they had a hit song called "Ready Or Not Here I Come". Which band wrote and released the original Soul version of this song in 1969 ?

15. What is the name of the band that "Ken Hensley" and "Lee Kerslake" were band mates in 1969 before joining "Uriah Heep" in early 1970s ?

16. Who was the drummer on the first "Jefferson Airplane" album "Jefferson Airplane Takes Off (1966)" which left the band right after recording and became the guitarist of "Moby Grape" ?

17. Before finally changing their name to "The Allman Brothers Band", they went through a few name changes. Which one of these names is not among them ?
    A. The Escorts
    B. The Allman Joys
    C. Second Coming
    D. The Hour Glass

18. Other than "Gary Rossington" and "Allen Collins", the third member of the triple guitar attack for "Lynyrd Skynyrd" was "Ed King". Which band he was coming from before joining "Lynyrd Skynyrd" ?

19. What is the last "Ten Years After" album that they released on "Deram" ?

20. Who was the only constant member of "Savoy Brown" since their formation in 1965 until his death in 2022 ?

21. What is the title of the first "ZZ Top" album that became a top ten hit and went gold ?

22. What is the name of the band that "Neil Young" and "Rick James" were band mates in 1966 ?

23. In 1965 Newport Folk Festival which band backed "Bob Dylan" when he went electric for the first time ?

24. Which band was "Al Kooper" a member of in 1966 before he formed "Blood, Sweat & Tears" in 1967 ?

25. What was the name of the "Jimi Hendrix" band in 1966 before he changed their name to "The Jimi Hendrix Experience" ?

26. What is the title of the first "Jethro Tull" hit in 1969 that featured "Martin Barre" as guitarist ?

27. What is the last "The Rolling Stones" album with "Brian Jones" as a band member ?

28. What is the first album by "John Mayall And The Blues Breakers" that "Mick Taylor" features on guitar ?

29. What was the last studio album by "Fleetwood Mac" which "Peter Green" played guitar in ?

30. What is the last album that "Tom Waits" recoded with "Asylum" ?

Chapter 6

1. The introduction to "Stairway To Heaven" by "Led Zeppelin" has been based on a song called "Taurus" which was written in 1968 and was included in the self-titled debut album by this band. What is the name of that band ?

2. Which song in the album "Highway 61 Revisited (1965)" by "Bob Dylan" features "Al Kooper" on keyboard ?

3. What is the title of the first "Tom Petty" solo album ?

4. What is the title of the album that "Neil Young" released right before joining "Crosby, Stills & Nash" ?

5. The first four "Jefferson Airplane" singles that "RCA" released didn't chart. What was the title of their fifth single but the first that charted ?

6. What was the first "The Allman Brothers Band" album that reached the Top Ten status in the charts ?

7. Which "Lynyrd Skynyrd" album became their first top ten hit ?

8. What is the title of the first "Alvin Lee" solo album that he released with "Mylon Lefevre" in 1973 before the first "Ten Years After" split ?

9. What is the last "ZZ Top" album that they released on the label "London" ?

10. Before releasing their first album in 1970, "Wishbone Ash" played their first gig as the opening act for which British Blues Rock band ?

11. What is the title of the first concept album by "Eloy" which they released in 1975 ?

12. The release of which single by "The Yardbirds" in 1965, resulted in "Eric Clapton" leaving the band due to differences in musical trajectory ?

13. What is the title of the first "Small Faces" album that they released on "Immediate" label ?

14. What is the name of the first "Canned Heat" guitarist and the band's founding member that formed the band alongside "Bob Hite" in 1965 ?

15. Which one of these bands was "Rod Argent" a member of before forming his own band "Argent" ?
    A. The Move
    B. The Kinks
    C. The Byrds
    D. The Zombies
    E. The Pretty Things
    F. The Electric Prunes

16. What is the title of the first "Van Morrison" album that he released with "Warner Bros." ?

17. Before forming "Free" in 1968, what was the name of the band that "Paul Rodgers" was a member of ?

18. What was the title of the last (Second) number one hit single by "Grand Funk Railroad" in 1974 ?

19. Which album featured the big single "Boom Boom" by "John Lee Hooker" ?

20. What is the title of the first "The Yardbirds" album that comprised of all original songs ?

21. What is the title of the only "The Yardbirds" album that featured both "Jeff Beck" and "Jimmy Page" ?

22. Before joining "The Rolling Stones" in 1974, which band was "Ron Wood" playing guitar in ?

23. What is the title of the last album that "J.J. Cale" released on "Shelter Records" ?

24. After leaving "Small Faces" in late 1968, which band did "Steve Marriott" formed with "Peter Frampton" ?

25. What is the title of the track that "The Yardbirds" played in the "Blow Up" movie ?

26. What is the title of the first single that "The Yardbirds" released right after "Jeff Beck" joined them in 1965 ?

27. Who is the only constant member of "Wishbone Ash" since 1970 until today ?

28. What is the first "ZZ Top" album that they released on "Warner Bros." ?

29. "Free Bird" by "Lynyrd Skynyrd" from their first album was a tribute to which person ?

30. What is the title of the first "The Allman Brothers Band" album that reached number one on the charts ?

CHAPTER 7

1. Who was the first actor to ever win three Oscars ?

2. One of the most important and influential western movies made by "John Ford" starring "John Wayne" in 1939 ?

3. Who played the main character "Monsieur Hulot" in the 1953 movie "Monsieur Hulot's Holiday" ?

4. In his last ever movie, "John Wayne" had a role alongside "James Stewart". Who's the director of that movie ?

5. The only actor/actress in the history of cinema with four Oscar wins ?

6. "Paul Newman" had this quote in one of his movies. "There is no sleep like the sleep of the innocent, while the wicked will never find rest." What's the title of that movie ?

7. Whose quote is this ? "In my profession if I trust too much, I won't celebrate many birthdays".

8. This 1971 German movie is about making a movie without the presence of the director, manuscript and enough money to continue the project in the beginning. What is the title of that movie ?

9. Which of the "Pier Paolo Pasolini" movies have this quote in it ? "The teachers should be killed and eaten".

10. This American director's career lasted just over two and a half decades with his last movie in 1948 called "Louisiana Story". What is the title of his first movie as a documentary which he directed in 1922 ?

11. Which movie "Ingrid Bergman" starred in that "Ingmar Bergman" directed ?

12. In this 1950 French movie, each character is involved with a character whom is involved with another character. This pattern continues throughout the movie until the last character gets involved in with the first character and thus the circle of love gets completed. What is the title of the movie ?

13. This actor had a role in the first ever movie that won the Oscars for the best picture, "Wings (1927)". He then became the two times Oscar winner as the Best Actor In a Leading Role in 1942 and 1953. Who is that actor ?

14. In how many movies did "Francois Truffaut" and "Jean-Pierre Leaud" work together ?

15. Which Oscar winning actor played in all of the following movies ?
    A. Local Hero (1983)
    B. Conversation Piece (1974)
    C. The Leopard (1963)
    D. Birdman Of Alcatraz (1962)
    E. Judgement At Nuremberg (1961)
    F. Sweet Smell Of Success (1957)
    G. Gunfight At The O.K. Corral (1957)
    H. From Here To Eternity (1953)
    I. The Flame And The Arrow (1950)

16. In the 1961 French movie directed by "Jean Pierre Melville", "Jean Paul Belmondo" plays the leading actor role as a clergyman. What is the title of the movie ?

17. In which "David Lynch" movie, "Isabella Rossellini" and "Dennis Hooper" had roles ?

18. What is the title of the Russian movie that shows the history of Russia by moving through a museum, has been directed by "Aleksandr Sokurov" and the whole movie has been filmed in one shot entirely ?

19. This Russian director made the movie "Earth" in 1930 about some Ukrainian village peasants that oppose the "Kulaks". Who is that director ?

20. Who is the Japanese director whose most notable movies have been named after either the seasons or the cities ?

21. This Indian director in his 1950s trilogy about a rural poor kid who grows up and moves to a big city, uses Ravi Shankar's music as the soundtrack of his movies. Who is that director ?

22. Who was the screenwriter of the 1961 "Alain Resnais" movie "Last Year At Marienbad" ?

23. What is the title of the 1964 Italian dark comedy directed by "Pietro Germi" about a pregnant teenage girl ?

24. With 14 years release difference, in 1944 and 1958, even though they were shot two years apart, these two "Sergei Eisenstein" movies depict the life of the 16th century Russian leader in two parts. What are the titles of the movies ?

25. What is the title of the 1943 "Henry King" movie, that "Jennifer Jones" received an Oscar for her portrayal of a rural girl ?

26. Who was the director of these three movies: "The Wizard Of Oz (1939)", "Gone With The Wind (1939)", and "Joan Of Arc (1948)" ?

27. Who was the producer of these three movies: "Gone With The Wind (1939)", "Rebecca (1940)", and "Duel In The Sun (1946)" ?

28. Which actor as one of the first Hollywood stars, played the role of "Robin Hood" in 1922 ?

29. Who was the first female star to officially place hand and footprints in the cement at "Chinese Theatre" in 1927 ?

30. Who was the first actor to ever win an Oscar for Best Actor category ?

CHAPTER 8

1. In 1949 for which movie did "John Huston" win two Oscars, one for best director and one for best writing ?

2. "Rome, Open City (1945)" and "Germany Year Zero (1948)" are two of the movies of "Roberto Rossellini"'s War Trilogy. What is the title of the third movie in this trilogy ?

3. "Burt Lancaster" and "Alain Delon" played in this 1963 movie directed by "Luchino Visconti". What is the title of the movie ?

4. As one of the First Ladies of Hollywood, she appeared in three of the most notable movies of D.W.Griffith : "The Birth Of A Nation (1915)", "Intolerance (1916)", and "Broken Blossoms (1919)". What is the name of this actress ?

5. In 1955 she played alongside "Bette Davis" in "The Virgin Queen" as one side of a love triangle. Who is this actress ?

6. The first version of this movie which is about a boxer was made in 1937, directed by "Michael Curtiz" and starring "Edward G. Robinson", "Bette Davis", and "Humphrey Bogart". The movie was remade in 1962 starring "Elvis Presley" and "Charles Bronson". What is the title of the movie ?

7. This 1984 Spoof Comedy about World War II was directed by "Zucker Brothers" and "Jim Abrahams". And starred "Val Kilmer" and "Omar Sharif". What is the title of the movie ?

8. In 1956 "Roger Vadim" movie "…And God Created Woman", which actress plays the main character ?

9. Which actor played in all of these movies:
"Rebel Without A Cause (1955)", "Giant (1956)", "Gunfight At The O.K. Corral (1957)", "The Trip (1967)", "Cool Hand Luke (1967)", "Easy Rider (1969)", "True Grit (1969)", "Apocalypse Now (1979)", and "Blue Velvet (1986)" ?

10. This Oscar nominated director has directed some of the relatively big budget movies in 1950s and 1960s including: "Gunfight At The O.K. Corral (1957)", "The Old Man And The Sea (1958)", "The Magnificent Seven (1960)", and "The Great Escape (1963)". What is the name of this director ?

11. Who was the first director to win an Oscar for Best Comedy Director for the 1927 movie "Two Arabian Knights" ?

12. Who was the director of the first movie that won Oscar for the Best Picture, "Wings (1927)" ?

13. In which 1934 movie directed by "Frank Capra", did "Clark Gable" play the main role and both of them won an Oscar for it ?

14. In how many movies did "Klaus Kinski" and "Werner Herzog" work together ?

15. Which movie did "Clint Eastwood" and "Jeff Bridges" play in, that "Michael Cimino" directed ?

16. In which 1950 Oscar winning movie directed by "Billy Wilder" did "William Holden" have a role ?

17. In 1959 he won an Oscar as he also was hosting the ceremony, for Best Actor In A Leading Role for the movie "Separate Tables (1958)" directed by "Delbert Mann". What is the name of this actor ?

18. Who was the director of the first movie to win the most Oscars with 11 in 1960 ?

19. The director of some of the big movies including: "Great Expectations (1946)", "Oliver Twist (1948)", and "The Bridge On The River Kwai (1957)" ?

20. Which one of these movies wasn't directed by "George Stevens" ?
    A. A Place In The Sun (1951)
    B. Shane (1953)
    C. From Here To Eternity (1953)
    D. Giant (1956)
    E. The Greatest Story Ever Told (1965)

21. Who was the first actress to ever win an Oscar ?

22. Which one of "Orson Welles" movies featured "Janet Leigh" as a star ?

23. Who is the director of these movies: "The Man In The White Suit (1951)", "The Ladykillers (1955)", and "Sweet Smell Of Success (1957)" ?

24. What was the first movie that "Dennis Hopper" played in ?

25. Who was the first director to ever win three Oscars ?

26. Which one of these movies was not directed by "Howard Hawks" ?
    A. Red River (1948)
    B. The Lost Weekend (1945)
    C. The Big Sleep (1946)
    D. To Have And Have Not (1944)
    E. Gentlemen Prefer Blondes (1953)
    F. Rio Bravo (1959)

27. Who is the director of these movies: "Sleuth (1972)", "Cleopatra (1963)", "Suddenly, Last Summer (1959)", "The Barefoot Contessa (1954)", "Julius Caesar (1953)", "All About Eve (1950)", "A Letter To Three Wives (1949)" ?

28. What was the first movie that "Shirley MacLaine" played in ?

29. Other than "Jack Nicholson" who is the only other actor who have received an Oscar nomination in every decade from 1960s to 2000s ?

30. In this 1939 "William Wyler" movie, "Laurence Olivier" as the main character received his first Oscar nomination.

CHAPTER 9

1. What is the title of the 1948 movie that "Laurence Olivier" both won the Oscar for Best Actor In A Leading Role and also directed the movie which won the Oscar for Best Picture ?

2. How many movies did "Elizabeth Taylor" and "Richard Burton" make together ?

3. Which one of these movies was directed by "Cecil B. DeMill" ?
    A. Ben Hur (1959)
    B. Spartacus (1960)
    C. The Ten Commandments (1956)
    D. Julius Caesar (1953)
    E. The Greatest Story Ever Told (1965)
    F. El Cid (1961)

4. In 1959 the musical "Gigi" won 9 Oscars including Best Director. Who directed that movie ?

5. In 1973 "Liza Minnelli" won an Oscar for her role in "Cabaret". Also the director of the movie won an Oscar for Best Director. Who was the director of the movie ?

6. Which one of these movies "Katharine Hepburn" didn't win an Oscar for ?
    A. The Philadelphia Story (1940)
    B. Morning Glory (1933)
    C. Guess Who's Coming To Dinner ? (1967)
    D. The Lion In Winter (1968)
    E. On Golden Pond (1981)

7. In which one of these movies "Anthony Quinn" didn't have a roll ?
    A. The Message (1976)
    B. Lost Command (1966)
    C. Lawrence Of Arabia (1962)
    D. The Guns Of Navarone (1961)
    E. The Bridge On The River Kwai (1957)
    F. The Hunchback Of Norte-Dame (1956)
    G. La Strada (1954)

8. Which one of these movies wasn't directed by "David Lean" ?
    A. Brief Encounter (1945)
    B. Great Expectations (1946)
    C. Oliver Twist (1948)
    D. Monkey Business (1952)
    E. The Bridge On The River Kwai (1957)
    F. Lawrence Of Arabia (1962)
    G. Doctor Zhivago (1965)

9. Which actress played in all of the following movies: "Conversation Piece (1974)", "Ludwig (1973)", "Death In Venice (1971)", "Teorema (1968)", "Oedipus Rex (1967)", "Ulysses (1954)", "Bitter Rice (1949)" ?

10. Which one of these movies wasn't directed by "Giuseppe Tornatore"?
    A. Malena (2000)
    B. The Legend Of 1900 (1998)
    C. Legends Of The Fall (1994)
    D. A Pure Formality (1994)
    E. Cinema Paradiso (1988)

11. In this 1943 movie based on a novel by "Ernest Hemingway" about the Spanish Civil War, "Gary Cooper" and "Ingrid Bergman" play together. What is the title of the movie?

12. Who is the director of these movies: "Little Women (1933)", "David Copperfield (1935)", "Romeo And Juliet (1936)", "The Philadelphia Story (1940)", "Gaslight (1944)", "A Star Is Born (1954)", "My Fair Lady (1964)"?

13. Who is the director of the following movies: "The Sandpiper (1965)", "Lust For Life (1956)", "The Bad And The Beautiful (1952)", "An American In Paris (1951)", "Father Of The Bride (1950)", "Madame Bovary (1949)", "Meet Me In St. Louis (1944)"?

14. In which one of these movies "Salvador Dali" collaborated with "Luis Bunuel"?
    A. That Obscure Object Of Desire (1977)
    B. The Phantom Of Liberty (1974)
    C. The Discreet Charm Of The Bourgeoisie (1972)
    D. The Milky Way (1969)
    E. Belle De Jour (1967)
    F. Dairy Of A Chambermaid (1964)
    G. The Exterminating Angel (1962)
    H. Land Without Bread (1933)
    I. L'Age D'Or (1930)

15. Which one of these movies wasn't directed by "Blake Edwards" ?
    A. Breakfast At Tiffany's (1961)
    B. Days Of Wine And Roses (1962)
    C. The Pink Panther (1963)
    D. A Shot In The Dark (1964)
    E. The Fortune Cookie (1966)
    F. The Party (1968)
    G. Victor/Victoria (1982)

16. Who was "Federico Fellini's" wife who had the leading female role in a few of his movies in 1950s and 1960s ?

17. Who is the director of the movie that got "Marlon Brando" nominated for his first Oscar in 1952 ?

18. Which actress had played in the following "Federico Fellini" movies: "The Clowns (1970)", "Boccaccio '70 (1962)" and "La Dolce Vita (1960)" ?

19. Who portrayed "Louis Pasteur" in 1936 movie "The Story Of Louis Pasteur" and "Emile Zola" in 1937 movie "The Life Of Emile Zola" ?

20. Which "John Schlesinger" movie features both "Dustin Hoffman" and "Laurence Olivier" ?

21. Who played in all of the following movies: "Voyage To The Bottom Of The Sea (1961)", "Around The World In 80 Days (1956)", "20000 Leagues Under The Sea (1954)", "Arsenic And Old Lace (1944)", "Casablanca (1942)", and "The Maltese Falcon (1941)" ?

22. Who was the first recipient of AFI (American Film Institute) Life Achievement Award in 1973 ?

23. Who is the director of these movies: "Kid Galahad (1937)", "The Adventures Of Robin Hood (1938)", "Angels With Dirty Faces (1938)", "Yankee Doodle Dandy (1942)", "Casablanca (1942)", "The Adventures Of Huckleberry Finn (1960)" ?

24. Who is the director of the following movies: "Presumed Innocent (1990)", "Sophie's Choice (1982)", "All The President's Men (1976)", and "Klute (1971)" ?

25. Who is the French director of the first feature film of "Beauty And The Beast (1946)" as well as "The Blood Of A Poet (1932)", "Orpheus (1950)", and "Testament Of Orpheus (1960)" ?

26. Which Oscar winning actress played in the following movies: "The Towering Inferno (1974)", "The Man In The Gray Flannel Suit (1956)", "Love Is A Many-Splendored Thing (1955)", "Carrie (1952)", "Madam Bovary (1949)", "Duel In The Sun (1946)", and "The Song Of Bernadette (1943)" ?

27. According to "Francois Truffaut", thanks to this French director "Nouvelle Vague (French New Wave)" started. Who is that director ?

28. Which French director made four movies in 1990s with the titles related to each season of the year with the format of "A Tale Of ..." ?

29. What was the first movie that "Clint Eastwood" directed ?

30. With which director did "Clint Eastwood" work in these movies: "Coogan's Bluff (1968)", "Two Mules For Sister Sara (1970)", "The Beguiled (1971)", "Dirty Harry (1971)", and "Escape From Alcatraz (1979)" ?

CHAPTER 10

1. Which one of these movies "William Holden" didn't play in ?
   A. Network (1976)
   B. The Towering Inferno (1974)
   C. The Wild Bunch (1969)
   D. The Guns Of Navarone (1961)
   E. The Bridge On The River Kwai (1957)
   F. Sabrina (1954)
   G. Stalag 17 (1953)
   H. Sunset Boulevard (1950)

2. For which movie did "Walter Matthau" win his only Oscar ?

3. Which directors co-directed the 1955 movie that "Jack Lemmon" won his first Oscar for ?

4. For which of their movies did "Joel Coen" and "Ethan Coen" win three Oscars ?

5. Who is the director of 1978 movie that "Jon Voight" won his Oscar for ?

6. Which one of these movies "Gene Hackman" didn't appear on ?
   A. The Royal Tenenbaums (2001)
   B. Wyatt Earp (1994)
   C. Unforgiven (1992)
   D. Glory (1989)
   E. Mississippi Burning (1988)
   F. Superman (1978)
   G. The Conversation (1974)
   H. The French Connection (1971)
   I. Bonnie And Clyde (1967)

7. Which one of these movies wasn't directed by "Fred Zinnemann" ?
   A. Pat Garrett And Billy The Kid (1973)
   B. A Man For All Seasons (1966)
   C. The Old Man And The Sea (1958)
   D. Oklahoma! (1955)
   E. From Here To Eternity (1953)
   F. High Noon (1952)

8. Which Oscar winning actor had played in all of the following movies: "Pat Garrett & Billy The Kid (1973)", "A Fistful Of Dynamite (1971)", "The Great Escape (1963)", and "The Magnificent Seven (1960)" ?

9. Who is the director of all of the following movies: "The Man Who Would Be King (1975)", "Moby Dick (1956)", "Moulin Rouge (1952)", "The African Queen (1951)", "Key Largo (1948)", "The Treasure Of The Sierra Madre (1948)", and "The Maltese Falcon (1941)" ?

10. Who is the director of the movie which "Olivia De Havilland" won her second Oscar for in 1950 ?

11. Who directed the following movies: "A Bridge Too Far (1977)", "Gandhi (1982)", "Cry Freedom (1987)", "Chaplin (1992)", and "Shadowlands (1993)" ?

12. Which one of these movies wasn't directed by "John Frankenheimer" ?
    A. Judgement At Nuremberg (1961)
    B. Birdman Of Alcatraz (1962)
    C. The Manchurian Candidate (1962)
    D. Seven Days In May (1964)
    E. The Train (1964)
    F. Seconds (1966)
    G. Grand Prix (1966)

13. In which Oscar winning "Sydney Pollack" movie "Robert Redford" and "Meryl Streep" play together ?

14. Who is the director of the movie that "Ingrid Bergman" won her third and last Oscar for in 1975 ?

15. What is the title of the first "Fritz Lang" American movie ?

16. Who is the director of the movie that "Audrey Hepburn" won her Oscar for in 1954 ?

17. Which one of the following movies wasn't directed by "William A. Wellman" ?
    A. Wings (1927)
    B. All Quiet On The Western Front (1930)
    C. The Public Enemy (1931)
    D. A Star Is Born (1937)
    E. Beau Geste (1939)
    F. The Ox-Bow Incident (1943)
    G. Story Of G.I. Joe (1945)

18. What is the title of the first movie that "John Huston" ever directed ?

19. For which movie did "George Stevens" win his first Oscar as Best Director in 1952 ?

20. Which Oscar winning actor played in the following movies: "The Ten Commandments (1956)", "Anastasia (1956)", "The Brothers Karamazov (1958)", "The Magnificent Seven (1960)", and "Taras Bulba (1962)" ?

21. Who was the director of the 1940 movie that "James Stewart" won his Oscar for ?

22. Which one of the following movies wasn't directed by "Elia Kazan" ?
    A. America America (1963)
    B. Splendor In The Grass (1961)
    C. East Of Eden (1955)
    D. Rebel Without A Cause (1955)
    E. On The Waterfront (1954)
    F. Viva Zapata! (1952)
    G. A Streetcar Named Desire (1951)
    H. Gentleman's Agreement (1947)
    I. A Tree Grows In Brooklyn (1945)

23. Who is the director of the 1942 movie "Yankee Doodle Dandy" that "James Cagney" won his Oscar for in 1943 ?

24. Which "Robert Benton" movie won the Oscar for Best Picture, Best Director, Best Actor In A Leading Role, Best Actress In A Supporting Role, And Best Writing in 1980 ?

25. Who is the director of the following movies: "The Secret Of Santa Vittoria (1969)", "Guess Who's Coming To Dinner (1967)", "It's A Mad, Mad, Mad, Mad World (1963)", "Judgement At Nuremberg (1961)", "Inherit The Wind (1960)", "The Defiant Ones (1958)" ?

26. What is the title of the notable 1938/1939 "Leslie Howard" movie that he both starred in and co-directed ?

27. In which "Michelangelo Antonioni" movie did "Alain Delon" have the role of the main character ?

28. Which actress won an Oscar for 1945 movie "Mildred Pierce" directed by "Michael Curtiz" ?

29. Who is the director of the following movies: "Vera Cruz (1954)", "Kiss Me Deadly (1955)", "Whatever Happened To Baby Jane ? (1962)", "Hush...Hush, Sweet Charlotte (1964)", "The Dirty Dozen (1967)", "Emperor Of The North (1973)" ?

30. Which actress played in all of the following movies: "The Thomas Crown Affair (1968)", "Little Big Man (1970)", "The Three Musketeers (1973)", "Chinatown (1974)", "The Towering Inferno (1974)", "Three Days Of The Condor (1975)", "Network (1976)", and "Arizona Dream (1993)" ?

CHAPTER 11

1. In which "Sydney Pollack" movie "Robert Redford" and "Faye Dunaway" play together ?

2. For which one of these movies did "William Holden" win his Oscar ?
   A. Sunset Boulevard (1950)
   B. Born Yesterday (1950)
   C. Stalag 17 (1953)
   D. Sabrina (1954)
   E. The Bridge On The River Kwai (1957)
   F. The Wild Bunch (1969)
   G. The Towering Inferno (1974)
   H. Network (1976)

3. Who directed the 1982 movie which "Ben Kingsley" won his Oscar for in 1983 ?

4. Who is the director of the following movies: "Laura (1944)", "Fallen Angel (1945)", "Where The Sidewalk Ends (1950)", "Angel Face (1952)", "The Man With The Golden Arm (1955)", "Anatomy Of A Murder (1959)", "Advise & Consent (1962)", "In Harm's Way (1965)" and "Bunny Lake Is Missing (1965)" ?

5. Which French director made the movie "Le Grand Melies" in 1952 as a tribute to one of the pioneers of filmmaking "George Melies" in the form of a biography of his life, starring the wife and son of "George Melies" ?

6. The last feature film that "Ronald Reagan" starred in alongside "Lee Marvin" and "John Cassavetes" was "The Killers (1964)". Who is the director of that movie ?

7. What is the title of the first "Jean-Luc Godard" movie that he used color widescreen stock ?

8. For which one of his movies did "Francois Truffaut" win Cannes Film Festival Best Director prize ?

9. "Scarlet Street" (1945) by "Fritz Lang" is a remake of the 1931 movie "La Chienne" by which French director ?

10. What is the title of the first feature film that "Jacques Tati" directed ?

11. After which one of "Roberto Rossellini" movies, he was invited to come to America by "David O. Selznick" ?

12. Which one of "Alain Resnais" movies was the first to be considered as a part of the "French New Wave" movement ?

13. What is the title of the first "Jean-Luc Godard" movie that "Alain Delon" starred in ?

14. Which one of these directors doesn't have a segment in "Boccaccio '70 (1962)" ?
    A. Federico Fellini
    B. Mario Monicelli
    C. Vittorio De Sica
    D. Pier Paolo Pasolini
    E. Luchino Visconti

15. Which Hollywood actress starred in the first American "Ernst Lubitsch" movie "Rosita (1923)" ?

16. Which one of these actors have not worked with "Elia Kazan" ?
    A. Gary Cooper
    B. Gregory Peck
    C. Spencer Tracy
    D. Jack Palance
    E. Anthony Quinn
    F. James Dean
    G. Marlon Brando
    H. Montgomery Clift
    I. Warren Beatty

17. In the movie "RoGoPaG (1962)" the "Pier Paolo Pasolini" section "La Ricotta" features one of the Hollywood director/actors as the main character. Who is that American director ?

18. Which one of "Luis Bunuel" movies won the Oscar for the Best Foreign Language Film ?

19. In the movie "Rome, Open City (1945)" directed by "Roberto Rossellini" who was the screenwriter, as well as the assistant director of his next movie "Paisan (1946)" ?

20. Who is the director of the following movies: "Under The Roofs Of Paris (1930)", "Le Million (1931)", "A Nous La Liberte (1931)", "Forever And A Day (1943)", "And Then There Were None (1945)", "Le Silence Est D'Or (1947)", and "The Beauty Of The Devil (1950)" ?

21. Who alongside "Jean-Luc Godard" formed "Dziga Vertov Group" in 1969 ?

22. Who is the director of the following movies: "IL Posto (1961)", "I Fidanzati (The Fiancés) (1963)", "Durante L'Estate (1971)", "The Tree Of Wooden Clogs (1978)", "Cammina, Cammina (1983)", "The Legend Of The Holy Drinker (1988)" ?

23. What is the title of the first "Federico Fellini" movie that won an Oscar for Best Foreign Language Picture ?

24. Who is the screenwriter of the following "Vittorio De Sica" movies: "A Brief Vacation (1973)", "Woman Times Seven (1967)", "Yesterday, Today And Tomorrow (1963)", "Boccaccio '70 (1962)", "Two Women (1960)", "Umberto D (1952)", "Miracle In Milan (1951)", "Bicycle Thieves (1948)", "Shoeshine (1946)", "The Children Are Watching Us (1942)" ?

25. What are the titles of the three movies that "Michelangelo Antonioni" made as a trilogy in 1960, 1961 and 1962 ?

26. Who is the director of the 1975 movie which was the second movie in the history of cinema that won five Oscars for all major categories: Best Picture, Best Director, Best Actor In A Leading Role, Best Actress In A Leading Role, and Best Writing, Screenplay ?

27. What is the title of the last "Federico Fellini" movie that won an Oscar for Best Foreign Language Film ?

28. What is the title of the last movie that "John Cassavetes" both directed and starred in alongside "Gena Rowlands" in 1984 ?

29. Which Oscar winning actor had played in all of the following movies: "Advise & Consent (1962)", "Spartacus (1960)", "Witness For The Prosecution (1957)", "Hobson's Choice (1954)", "O. Henry's Full House (1952)", "The Blue Veil (1951)", "The Big Clock (1948)", "This Land Is Mine (1943)", "Tales Of Manhattan (1942)", "The Hunchback Of Norte Dame (1939)", "Mutiny On The Bounty (1935)", "Les Miserables (1935)", and "The Private Life Of Henry VIII (1933)" ?

30. In which one of these movies "Montgomery Clift" didn't play ?
    A. Double Indemnity (1944)
    B. Red River (1948)
    C. The Heiress (1949)
    D. A Place In The Sun (1951)
    E. From Here To Eternity (1953)
    F. Suddenly, Last Summer (1959)
    G. Wild River (1960)
    H. Judgement At Nuremberg (1961)

CHAPTER 12

1. Who is the director of the following movies: "Is Paris Burning ? (1966)", "The Day And The Hour (1963)", "Purple Noon (1960)", "Gervaise (1956)", "Forbidden Games (1952)", "La Bataille Du Rail (1946)" ?

2. For which one of his movies did "Francois Truffaut" win his Oscar for Best Foreign Language Film ?

3. What is the title of the first movie that "Roberto Rossellini" and "Ingrid Bergman" made together ?

4. What is the title of the movie that "Elia Kazan" won his first Oscar for as the Best Director ?

5. What is the title of the last movie that "Luis Bunuel" ever directed ?

6. What is the title of the first movie that "Federico Fellini" ever directed ?

7. What is the title of the movie that brought "Robert Bresson" his international reputation ?

8. Who is the director of the following movies: "Leibelei (1933), "Letter From An Unknown Woman (1948)", "La Ronde (1950)", "Le Plaisir (1952)", "The Earrings Of Madam De... (1953)", "Lola Montes (1955)" ?

9. What is the title of the first movie that brought "Alfred Hitchcock" international attention in 1934 which he remade it in 1956 ?

10. What is the title of the most notable movie by french director "Abel Gance" ?

11. What is the title of the first American "F.W. Murnau" movie ?

12. Who is the director of the following movies: "The Beekeeper (1986)", "Landscape In The Mist (1988)", "Ulysses' Gaze (1995)", "Eternity And A Day (1998)", "The Weeping Meadow (2004)" ?

13. What is the title of the first movie that "Sidney Lumet" ever directed ?

14. What is the title of the first "Pier Paolo Pasolini" movie that he wrote and directed about the struggles of a pimp ?

15. Who is the director of the following movies: "The Student Prince In Old Heidelberg (1927)", "Broken Lullaby (1932)", "Trouble In Paradise (1932)", "Ninotchka (1939)", "The Shop Around The Corner (1940)", "To Be Or Not To Be (1942)", and "Heaven Can Wait (1943)" ?

16. What is the title of the first coloured "Federico Fellini" movie ?

17. What is the name of the British director who directed the following movies: "Oh! What A Lovely War (1969)", "A Bridge Too Far (1977)", "Gandhi (1982)", "Cry Freedom (1987)", "Chaplin (1992)", "Shadowlands (1993)" ?

18. What is the title of the last movie that "Cecil B. DeMille" ever directed which was also the title of the same movie that he first made in 1923 ?

19. Which one of these "Vittorio De Sica" movies didn't win an Oscar for Best Foreign Language Film ?
    A. Shoeshine (1946)
    B. Bicycle Thieves (1948)
    C. Yesterday, Today And Tomorrow (1963)
    D. Marriage Italian Style (1964)
    E. The Garden Of The Finzi-Continis (1970)

20. Which big Italian director collaborated with "Federico Fellini" on the script of his 1952 movie "The White Sheik" ?

21. What is the title of the first "David Lean" movie that he directed outside of England ?

22. Which "Robert Bresson" movie was inspired by "Crime And Punishment" by "Fyodor Dostoevsky" ?

23. What is the title of the first American "Alfred Hitchcock" movie ?

24. In which one of "John Huston" movies, he casted his own father which resulted in both of them winning Oscars ?

25. The movie "The Children's Hour (1961)" by "William Wyler" is the remake of one of his own movies that he made 25 years prior. What is the title of that movie ?

26. What is the title of the first "Billy Wilder" movie starring "Marilyn Monroe" ?

27. What is the title of the first "Federico Fellini" movie starring "Marcello Mastroianni" ?

28. In which one of his movies did "Pier Paolo Pasolini" cast his own mother in the role of "Virgin Mary" ?

29. What is the title of the first "Alain Resnais" English language movie ?

30. Which Oscar winning actor had played in all of the following movies: "The Citadel (1938)", "Night Train To Munich (1940)", "Blithe Spirit (1945)", "The Ghost And Mrs. Muir (1947)", "Unfaithfully Yours (1948)", "Cleopatra (1963)", "My Fair Lady (1964)", and "The Agony And The Ecstasy (1965)" ?

Answers To The Questions In Chapter 1

1. Sign Language
2. Linda Perry
3. While My Guitar Gently Weeps
4. Gaucho (1980)
5. You Keep Me Hangin' On
6. Super Freak
7. Eric Woolfson
8. Bobby Blue Bland
9. Savoy Brown
10. Elephant's Memory
11. Indian Summer
12. Herb Alpert
13. Arthur Crudup
14. Attila
15. Flaming Youth
16. The Felicity
17. Bobby Blue Bland
18. Willie Dixon
19. Three
20. B. Ian Curtis
21. Spooky Tooth
22. Tim Hardin
23. Otis Rush
24. The Paramounts
25. Skid Row
26. I'd Rather Go Blind
27. Tom & Jerry
28. Buddy Guy
29. Hindu Love Gods
30. Tammi Terrell

Answers To The Questions In Chapter 2

1. A. Whitesnake
2. .38 Special
3. Keith Relf
4. Howard Devoto
5. Shiloh
6. Delaney & Bonnie
7. The New Christy Minstrels
8. Stone The Crows
9. Wizzard
10. Fred Neil
11. Junior Wells
12. Sandy Denny
13. Johnny Copeland
14. Cozy Powell
15. F. Mind Garage
16. A. Beggars Banquet (1968)
17. D. Nowhere Man
18. Takin' It To The Streets (1976)
19. Freddie King
20. Captain Beyond
21. Episode Six
22. D. Ronnie James Dio
23. Albert King
24. Joe Cocker
25. E. Octopus's Garden
26. Jeff Lynne
27. A. Bob Dylan
28. The Bob Seger System
29. Aynsley Dunbar
30. B.B. King In London (1971)

Answers To The Questions In Chapter 3

1. Cream Of The Crop (1969)
2. My Happiness
3. The Primettes
4. The Jays
5. Paul Simon
6. Earth
7. A. Aretha Franklin
8. Full House (1970)
9. The Wilde Flowers
10. Days Of The Future Passed (1967)
11. Matching Mole
12. What'd I Say
13. Maybellene
14. The Kinks
15. The Golliwogs
16. Nursery Cryme (1971)
17. The Lamb Lies Down On Broadway (1974)
18. The League Of Gentlemen
19. Pure Prairie League
20. Dire Straits
21. Johnny Cash
22. Streetwalkers
23. The City
24. Ike Turner
25. D. Blue Cheer
26. The Leathercoated Minds
27. David Coverdale
28. Tony Joe White
29. F. Willie Nelson
30. Nashville Skyline (1969)

Answers To The Questions In Chapter 4

1. C. Rainbow
2. Rod Evans
3. Willie Dixon
4. B. B.B. King
5. The V.I.P.s
6. Daevid Allen
7. E. The Strawbs
8. Thirds (1971)
9. Electric Pigeons
10. The Falcons
11. The Afghan Whigs
12. Ol' '55
13. Mercury Rev
14. The Boys Next Door
15. Peter Green
16. Car Wheels On A Gravel Road (1998)
17. The Pretty Things
18. 1960
19. Blodwyn Pig
20. Fleetwood Mac (1975)
21. Armageddon
22. The Ravens
23. Fotheringay
24. The Groundhogs
25. O. V. Wright
26. The Notorious Byrd Brothers (1968)
27. Sticky Fingers (1971)
28. A Hard Road (1967)
29. Kiln House (1970)
30. The Vagrants

Answers To The Questions In Chapter 5

1. Bette Midler
2. Aftermath (1966)
3. Carry It On (1971)
4. Benefit (1970)
5. Muswell Hillbillies (1971)
6. High And Mighty (1976)
7. Rising Sons
8. Now And Them (1967)
9. Highway 61 Revisited (1965)
10. The Warlocks
11. Noel Redding
12. Let Me Up (I've Had Enough) (1987)
13. Heart Of Gold
14. The Delfonics
15. Toe Fat
16. Alexander (Skip) Spence
17. C. Second Coming
18. Strawberry Alarm Clock
19. Watt (1970)
20. Kim Simmonds
21. Tres Hombres (1973)
22. The Mynah Birds
23. The Paul Butterfield Blues Band
24. The Blues Project
25. Jimmy James & The Blue Flames
26. Living In The Past
27. Beggars Banquet (1968)
28. Crusade (1967)
29. Then Play On (1969)
30. Heartattack And Vine (1980)

Answers To The Questions In Chapter 6

1. Spirit
2. Like A Rolling Stone
3. Full Moon Fever (1989)
4. Everybody Knows This Is Nowhere (1969)
5. Somebody To Love (1967)
6. Eat A Peach (1972)
7. Nuthin' Fancy (1975)
8. On The Road To Freedom (1973)
9. Tejas (1976)
10. The Aynsley Dunbar Retaliation
11. Power And The Passion (1975)
12. For Your Love
13. There Are But Four Small Faces (1967)
14. Alan Wilson
15. D. The Zombies
16. Astral Weeks (1968)
17. Brown Sugar
18. The Loco-Motion
19. Burnin' (1962)
20. Roger The Engineer(Yardbirds) (1966)
21. Blow Up (1967)
22. Faces
23. 5 (1979)
24. Humble Pie
25. Stroll On
26. Heart Full Of Soul
27. Andy Powell
28. Deguello (1979)
29. Duane Allman
30. Brothers And Sisters (1973)

Answers To The Questions In Chapter 7

1. Walter Brennan
2. Stagecoach (1939)
3. Jacques Tati
4. Don Siegel
5. Katharine Hepburn
6. A New Kind Of Love (1963)
7. John Wayne
8. Beware Of A Holy Whore (1971)
9. The Hawks And The Sparrows (1966)
10. Nanook Of The North (1922)
11. Autumn Sonata (1978)
12. La Ronde (1950)
13. Gary Cooper
14. Seven
15. Burt Lancaster
16. Leon Morin, Priest (1961)
17. Blue Velvet (1986)
18. Russian Ark (2002)
19. Aleksandr Dovzhenko
20. Yasujiro Ozu
21. Satyajit Ray
22. Alain Robbe-Grillet
23. Seduced And Abandoned (1964)
24. Ivan The Terrible, Part I (1944), Ivan The Terrible, Part II (1958)
25. The Song Of Bernadette (1943)
26. Victor Fleming
27. David O. Selznick
28. Douglas Fairbanks
29. Mary Pickford
30. Emil Jannings

Answers To The Questions In Chapter 8

1. The Treasure Of The Sierra Madre (1948)
2. Paisan (1946)
3. The Leopard (1963)
4. Lillian Gish
5. Joan Collins
6. Kid Galahad (1962)
7. Top Secret! (1984)
8. Brigitte Bardot
9. Dennis Hopper
10. John Sturges
11. Lewis Milestone
12. William A. Wellman
13. It Happened One Night (1934)
14. Five
15. Thunderbolt And Lightfoot (1974)
16. Sunset Boulevard (1950)
17. David Niven
18. William Wyler
19. David Lean
20. C. From Here To Eternity (1953)
21. Janet Gaynor
22. Touch Of Evil (1958)
23. Alexander Mackendrick
24. Rebel Without A Cause (1955)
25. Frank Capra
26. B. The Lost Weekend (1945)
27. Joseph L. Mankiewicz
28. The Trouble With Harry (1955)
29. Michael Caine
30. Wuthering Heights (1939)

Answers To The Questions In Chapter 9

1. Hamlet (1948)
2. Eleven
3. C. The Ten Commandments (1956)
4. Vincent Minnelli
5. Bob Fosse
6. A. The Philadelphia Story (1940)
7. E. The Bridge On The River Kwai (1957)
8. D. Monkey Business (1952)
9. Silvana Mangano
10. C. Legends Of The Fall (1994)
11. For Whom The Bell Tolls (1943)
12. George Cukor
13. Vincente Minnelli
14. I. L'Age D'Or (1930)
15. E. The Fortune Cookie (1966)
16. Giulietta Masina
17. Elia Kazan
18. Anita Ekberg
19. Paul Muni
20. Marathon Man (1976)
21. Peter Lorre
22. John Ford
23. Michael Curtiz
24. Alan J. Pakula
25. Jean Cocteau
26. Jennifer Jones
27. Jacques Rivette
28. Eric Rohmer
29. Play Misty For Me (1971)
30. Don Siegel

Answers To The Questions In Chapter 10

1. D. The Guns Of Navarone (1961)
2. The Fortune Cookie (1966)
3. John Ford, Mervyn LeRoy and Joshua Logan
4. No Country For Old Men (2007)
5. Hal Ashby
6. D. Glory (1989)
7. A. Pat Garrett And Billy The Kid (1973)
8. James Coburn
9. John Huston
10. William Wyler
11. Richard Attenborough
12. A. Judgement At Nuremberg (1961)
13. Out Of Africa (1985)
14. Sidney Lumet
15. Fury (1936)
16. William Wyler
17. B. All Quiet On The Western Front (1930)
18. The Maltese Falcon (1941)
19. A Place In The Sun (1951)
20. Yul Brynner
21. George Cukor
22. D. Rebel Without A Cause (1955)
23. Michael Curtiz
24. Kramer Vs. Kramer (1979)
25. Stanley Kramer
26. Pygmalion (1938/39)
27. L'eclisse (1962)
28. Joan Crawford
29. Robert Aldrich
30. Faye Dunaway

Answers To The Questions In Chapter 11

1. Three Days Of The Condor (1975)
2. C. Stalag 17 (1953)
3. Richard Attenborough
4. Otto Preminger
5. Georges Franju
6. Don Siegel
7. A Woman Is A Woman (1961)
8. The 400 Blows (1959)
9. Jean Renoir
10. Jour De Fete (1949)
11. Rome, Open City (1945)
12. Hiroshima Mon Amour (1959)
13. Nouvelle Vague (1990)
14. D. Pier Paolo Pasolini
15. Mary Pickford
16. A. Gary Cooper
17. Orson Welles
18. The Discreet Charm Of The Bourgeoisie (1972)
19. Federico Fellini
20. Rene Clair
21. Jean-Pierre Gorin
22. Ermanno Olmi
23. La Strada (1954)
24. Cesare Zavattini
25. L'Avventura (1960), La Notte (1961), L'Eclisse (1962)
26. Milos Forman
27. Amarcord (1973)
28. Love Streams (1984)
29. Charles Laughton
30. A. Double Indemnity (1944)

Answers To The Questions In Chapter 12

1. Rene Clement
2. Day For Night (1973)
3. Stromboli (1949)
4. Gentleman's Agreement (1947)
5. That Obscure Object Of Desire (1977)
6. Variety Lights (1950)
7. Dairy Of A Country Priest (1950)
8. Max Ophuls
9. The Man Who Knew Too Much (1934)
10. Napoleon (1927)
11. Sunrise : A Story Of Two Humans (1927)
12. Theo Angelopoulos
13. 12 Angry Men (1957)
14. Accattone (1961)
15. Ernst Lubitsch
16. Juliet Of The Spirits (1965)
17. Richard Attenborough
18. The Ten Commandments (1956)
19. D. Marriage Italian Style (1964)
20. Michelangelo Antonioni
21. The Bridge On The River Kwai (1957)
22. Pickpocket (1959)
23. Rebecca (1940)
24. The Treasure Of The Sierra Madre (1948)
25. These Three (1936)
26. The Seven Year Itch (1955)
27. La Dolce Vita (1960)
28. The Gospel According to St. Matthew (1964)
29. Providence (1977)
30. Rex Harrison

www.ingramcontent.com/pod-product-compliance
Lightning Source LLC
Chambersburg PA
CBHW020421150626
46554CB00014B/2322